I Trust Time

by Ivan Echemendia

"Even silence, when felt deeply enough, becomes a voice."

Opening Page.

Opening Page.

People live and act in ignorance of the fact that life is a compilation of moments marked by our actions, making our path here on earth a vivid butterfly event in which every small choice or event we do may have a unique, vast, and cosmic outcome on the future. Even though knowing that, they proceed regardless, thinking that a final judgment will come and a divine mercy will be granted, forsaking and forgiving all their sins.

This book is not written to impress, not written to overshadow others. I'm not a writer by trade, but I'm a soul - a mass of energy being real, speaking out loud, trying to be heard by a world that doesn't seem to value the real purpose of life. I'm writing to those who need to feel less alone, people that I must believe exist, out of the billions of inhabitants on this giant mass of matter floating in an infinite darkness we call planet Earth -including myself.

It is made from really long daily rides in my beloved and so-called safe place, inside the cab of my car - just me and the humming sound of the engine. A sound only compared to the brave sailors being dragged by the sirens' songs. A connection felt so deeply that every noise from the outside fades beneath the waves of silence emerging from within me. It was made from long nights of self- reflection, overthinking every action made and yet to be made. Nights that phased all logic of physics and time itself, as if the clock stopped ticking - like the sand stopped falling from the hourglass, an infinite ocean of thoughts running endlessly like rivers into their destined sea.

It was written in places no one saw me hurting - maybe because I chose them carefully, or maybe because the rest of the world simply doesn't care. A world where appearances matter more than truth.

You'll find pain here - pain like billions of shards of broken glass sharpened like ancient katanas, piercing a heart into grains of sand. You'll find the truth of being trapped in the wrong space, the wrong time. Of surviving a hostile era, feeling like you were born in the wrong decade, maybe even the wrong century. Like a single grain of sand lost in an endless desert.

And yet - there will also be moments where you feel seen, even if you've never met me.

Recognition to:

To grandparents who raised two generations. To a mother assigned the role of both mother and father, who proved that God gives the toughest battles to His strongest warriors.

And to the five voices who reminded me I still had something worth building. May you one day know what you meant to someone who never stopped believing in you.

It's not for fame. Not to shine. But to be felt.

Chapter 1- Born in the Wrong Time.

Chapter 1- Born in the Wrong Time.

What is time?

To really understand everything, there is no better starting point than this question. Just like the Big Bang gave birth to the universe, I believe our existence has evolved from something so small into something vast - and yet, I question if we've truly evolved. Because from my point of view, evolution isn't about fashion, automobiles, rockets to space, money, or power. If we really analyze it, isn't that kind of evolution what's slowly pushing us toward extinction?

True evolution comes from the soul - from the mind, from our inner energy, from the aura we each carry. And for reasons I can't explain, that evolution is ignored in today's world. Maybe I'm shrinking "time" too much by measuring it in days, when it's better reflected across centuries.

My era.

I've never quite belonged here - not in this time, not in this world shaped by noise and speed. While people my age chased trends and trophies, I watched from the edges, wondering if maybe I was dropped into the wrong decade... or the wrong century entirely. There's always been this ache in me - not fear, but a quiet weight, like my soul is out of sync with the rhythm of everything around me. I didn't grow up with answers. I grew up with questions - and silence. The kind of silence that teaches you to listen to your own *heartbeat... because no one else can hear it.*

What kind of world do we live in that turns young people - even children -into souls who question their worth? I've only walked this Earth for two and a half decades, and I've felt that pain. The kind of pain that doesn't leave. The kind that, no matter how hard I try to silence it, keeps burning in the last pieces of my heart and echoing through my subconscious.

In this era, the more you give to the world, the less you seem to receive. It's a generation that expects but doesn't provide - not kindness, not sincerity, not love. Unless there's something to gain, people don't offer anything at all. We're surrounded by hypocrisy, fake smiles, toxic connections. We've become leeches - feeding off others' light until they have nothing left. I've learned - some the hard way - that there's no worse blind person than one who chooses not to see.

People know they're hurting you. They know what they're doing. But they keep going.

We live in a time of chaos and speed. No one looks up at the stars anymore. No one takes time to appreciate the beauty of existence or the fragility of life. People don't say "I love you" to their mothers, their grandparents - not because they don't feel it, but because the world doesn't slow down enough to let them say it. And then, one day, it's too late.

We live on fast-forward - until the moment death taps our shoulder and reminds us we should've pressed pause.

And when that moment comes, the regret cuts like a saw through bone. You wish you had one more night, one more Sunday dinner, one more moment to tell the people who truly mattered that you loved them - not for what they gave you, but for simply existing beside you.

This world worships noise. The louder you are, the more people pay attention - no matter how toxic or empty your message is. The truth has become a whisper. Silence is mistaken for weakness. People scream just to feel real. They drown in the echo of their own false reflections. Even children mimic what they see, repeating the chaos without understanding it. And we wonder why things are falling apart.

Money erases guilt. Power buries consequences. People trade morals for clout. And slowly, they lose the ability to recognize their own shadow. It's like living in a ghost town. Everyone's shouting, but no one's saying anything. We're souls drifting across a planet that doesn't remember what it means to feel. And for people like me - people who want to live honestly - the world seems unlivable. Life is like music. More like a band. And every instrument has to stay in rhythm. But when even one falls out of sync, the song collapses. That's how I feel in this time - out of rhythm with the world.

The ones who could change it are ignored. The ones who could do good are too busy chasing power. Wars are prioritized over peace. Innocent people are treated like criminals, and the people meant to protect us are often the ones misusing their power.

We all know this planet is dying - yet we pretend we don't. Children starve while the world turns its head. Medicine exists, but the poor die without it. And why? Because they're not "one of us."

But aren't we all human?

We're in an age where people care more about your bank account than your heart. They care more about your car than your story. Emotional connection is transactional. You have to earn basic love. And still, people wonder why we're falling apart.

We search for life on other planets while ignoring the life we've destroyed on this one. What's the point of discovering a new galaxy if we've lost our humanity back home?

What is time? (For the mind)

Time is a measurement - a system we created to track motion, change, aging, the rise and fall of everything around us. Seconds, minutes, hours... they help us organize the chaos. But in truth? Time isn't a clock.

It's a river - always moving forward, never stopping, even when we wish it would.

What is time? (For the soul)

Time is the space between who you are and who you're meant to become. It's the silence between heartbeats, the weight behind every "what if," the quiet rhythm of becoming - even when no one sees it.

It's the nights where minutes feel like eternities, and the years that vanish in a blink.

Time doesn't speak - but it teaches.

It teaches us through loss... Through waiting...Through those moments where all we want is to go back, or fast forward, or stop everything and just breathe. But time doesn't stop.

It asks us to move with it.

To carry our pain, our hope, our dreams - and walk forward anyway. And maybe that's what time really is...

A test.

Not of how long we live...but of what we do with the time we're given.

Time is one of the most powerful, mysterious forces we'll never truly hold.

It's not just clocks or calendars - it's the invisible thread that ties our memories, choices, dreams, and regrets into a single story.

Time is the weight in your chest when a moment passes too fast... And the aching drag when pain refuses to end.

It's the quiet reminder that everything ends, but also the proof that everything can begin again. To some, time is the enemy - a thief. To others, it's a gift - a path.

But to souls like mine, time isn't something to count. It's something to feel.

To mark with meaning. To transform into legacy. Live every moment as it is given.

Spend as much time as you can with the people who matter - your friend, your partner, your family. Say "I love you" while you can. Face the world even in its brokenness, and still choose to be good. Do good, even when they don't deserve it. Because at the end of the day, life is a loan. We are all playing with borrowed time. And we don't know when it's due.

So while you're here... live. Really live. And to the ones who drain others, who hurt without remorse?

Karma is a chameleon.

You may not see it,

but it's watching.

Chapter 2- Where Thunder Never Spoke, Echoes Learned to Sing.

Chapter 2- Where Thunder Never Spoke, Echoes Learned to Sing.

As time has shown me, there is mysticism and beauty in the existence of everything we know and everything we've yet to imagine. An action, a reaction - they say.

Water from lakes and oceans evaporates, rises to touch the sky, then falls back to Earth as torrential rain under thunderclouds dark as a blackout in New York City. Lightning cuts the sky open.

Thunder roars like a god clearing its throat. The strongest among us retreat to shelter, and the rain begins - pouring endlessly, carving dry earth into rivers, rivers into waterfalls, and then back to ocean, until the sun rises once again, tracing the sky with a rainbow.

Even our planet came from somewhere - a galaxy inside a universe birthed by the Big Bang. And every great force, even death itself, had to begin somewhere before becoming the reaper we now fear. Everything in this life has a beginning. A childhood. Even me.

I don't remember the first time I felt pain - not the kind that scrapes your knee, but the kind that settles quietly in the soul and never fully leaves. What I do remember is the silence. I was a quiet child, not because I didn't have things to say, but because I didn't think the world wanted to hear them. I learned early that people don't always listen - not to the quiet ones, not to the soft hearts. So I paid attention instead.

To faces. To footsteps. To moods that shifted like weather. I grew up not in a world of loud joy or noisy chaos, but in the in-between - a space where I learned to read emotions like survival, and carry weight that no one ever saw. There was love, yes - deep, selfless love from the ones who raised me. But even that love had to fight through the noise of the world outside, and the heaviness that already lived inside me.

Every sound is powerful enough, but not every echo stays silenced forever. Every child has a dream - astronaut, firefighter, explorer. I had mine, too. But I also had a moment. My family wasn't perfect, and like any polished structure, there were cracks between the walls. My parents weren't always happy together. My birth was a surprise to my father's family, and my mother and I never fully belonged there. Eventually, he left - confused or perhaps easily influenced. He abandoned the woman who brought his child into the world. But she wasn't truly alone. I was there. And so were my grandparents. Together, they showed me what it meant to stick together, and they poured into my bones the quiet strength I carry today.

Family, I learned, is like concrete - at first soft and formless, but with time, it hardens into the foundation of everything.

After my father's departure, everything changed. My mom became both parents. And at five years old, I became "the man of the house." She worked tirelessly to *keep us afloat. And I? I became the silent one, the sharp-eyed one, the dreamer. Not the kid riding bikes or running through*

sprinklers, but the one who stayed in the classroom during breaks, staring into space like he was flying his own rocket to the moon - to save humanity... and most of all, to save my mom.

I overthought everything, analyzed every step, avoiding risks others rushed into. I spent long hours in rooms where the only sound was the echo of my desperation to be seen.

But every journey has its turning point. For me, innocence began to slip away when I realized the world - and the people in it - weren't always kind. One moment that still lives in me happened in middle school. My teacher, Ms.

Milagros, was brilliant, selfless, and kind beyond words. She taught me life, morals, and meaning. One day, she returned from a meeting looking distant, her head down. My classmates were too lost in their own worlds to notice. But I saw her. I followed quietly and overheard a conversation with another teacher. She was being let go - the Department of Education couldn't pay her in her final months before retirement. If she wanted to stay, she'd have to work for free. Still, she said, "I won't abandon them. They're my children."

I couldn't hold it. I ran to her, crying, pretending to feel sick - just to be close to her, to remind her someone needed her. She took me to class, unaware of what I'd heard. But inside me, something broke. What innocence I had left drained from me that day like thunder shaking loose the last clouds in the sky.

Without a paternal figure, my mother and I eventually moved in with my maternal grandparents. My grandmother, a retired school director, celebrated my birthday like it was a national holiday. Her cakes were baked with love and her presence gave warmth I can still feel. She read the Bible to me, took me to church, and taught me kindness through action. My grandfather was my role model - honorable, moral, brilliant.

He played with me, taught me to cook (a passion I still carry), and took me to museums to teach me history. In a short time, he became a compass I still follow. But that season ended too soon. In 2008, my grandparents and uncle flew to Miami, leaving Cuba behind. That airport goodbye is etched into my soul. I was only eight, waving goodbye, my heart pounding like war

drums in a battlefield of silence. When my grandfather broke eye contact and walked through that gate, I felt time freeze. I couldn't speak. I cried for days. It was the first time I felt a forever kind of sadness.

From then on, it was just me and my mom. She lost her parents and brother. I lost my foundations. And she got sick - often, and seriously. Some days, she couldn't stand. Once, she nearly became paralyzed after a fall. I took care of the house, our dog, her medicine, everything. Two people - friends of my grandmother - helped us survive. For five long years, I carried more than a child should ever be asked to.

But time passed. And like a seagull flying over an ocean, our family came back together. That reunion, years later, remains one of the most emotional moments of my life.

Every moment - every birthday, every sickness, every goodbye - shaped me. That quiet, observant, dreaming little boy became the man I am now: someone who values loyalty, honesty, and keeping one's word above all else. A man who gives to the world without expecting anything in return. A man who understands that you can't save those who don't want saving - but also refuses to give up on the ones who do.

That child still lives in me. He still climbs into that imaginary rocket when the world feels too heavy. He still dreams of salvation - for the world, for the people he loves, and for the voices that once reminded him he was never truly alone.

He is me. A boy, a dreamer in a world -

Where Thunder Never Spoke, Echoes Learned to Sing.

Chapter 3 - Where Thunder Was Silent, and Shadows Learned to Fight.

Chapter 3 - Where Thunder Was Silent, and Shadows Learned to Fight.

Good and evil. Day and night. Yin and Yang. Our lives are walking evidence that everything in existence has its opposite. In a world bursting with freedom, identity, and technological advance, the soul has become an endangered species. This era- fast, loud, and endlessly connected-can be devastating for pure-hearted people.

Souls that were once open to wonder risk being corrupted by silence, loneliness, and exposure to the wrong light.

People fear the machine, the AI, the future. But we should fear the ones who made them. Because it's not the tools that twist us-it's the pain we've buried, the voids we never filled.

All it takes is a moment. One moment. One damaged, lonely soul. And suddenly, you're not walking through life-you're falling. And you don't even know it.

They say silence is peace. But I've learned silence can also be a battlefield. Not every war is fought with weapons. Some are waged in the shadows of your own mind-behind locked doors, under soft ceilings, in quiet hours when no one is watching.

I lived most of my early life surrounded by noise-yet haunted by loneliness. Not the kind you feel when you're alone... but the kind that sits next to you, even in a room full of people. The kind that makes your chest echo, because your heart is the only thing making sound.

And somewhere in that silence, something began to grow inside me-something no one saw. It started as curiosity. Then comfort. Then habit. Then hunger. Not for love. Not for connection. For escape.

I created my own demon. Not with intention... but with loneliness. I fed it silently. I protected it with shame. And I wore a mask the world could never see through. No one knew that every night was a quiet war. A war between the boy who wanted to be clean... and the boy who just wanted to feel something. But here's the thing about demons born in silence: they grow in darkness. And I? I decided to become light.

Every demon has a beginning. Mine was born in my early years, a place where innocence masked the danger. A time when people didn't look closely, didn't take the warning signs seriously, because-after all-I was

"just a kid." That's where it began. That's when it crept in.

What started as innocent curiosity evolved into something more dangerous. The demon wasn't just in my home. It lived in my head, in my hands, in my shadow. It fed off my silence and wore a disguise of relief.

The loneliness didn't scare me anymore-it became my comfort. My preferred state. I didn't want to be seen, because being seen meant being known. And being known meant being judged.

Eventually, I realized I wasn't the one in control anymore. The demon was.

So what do you do when you realize you've been carrying something for years- something no one else can see? What do you do when your own shadow becomes your enemy?

You begin to fight.

Not with noise. Not with blame. But with awareness.

I carried that demon through two decades of life. I carried it in silence, ashamed of a war no one even knew I was fighting. I wasn't committing crimes. I wasn't hurting anyone. But I was hurting myself. Because the boy I wanted to become- the man I'm becoming-deserved to be free. And freedom starts with truth.

I won't let this demon pass to my children. I won't let it stain the legacy I'm trying to build. I've seen the Leviathan-the ancient monster of the soul-and I've looked it in the eye. It told me I'd never win. That I'd always come back to it. That I was too weak.

But that's when I found my reason. Some people find theirs in faith. Others in family. I found mine in five voices. Five lights in a cold world. Five reasons to fight harder than I ever have. They didn't even know they were saving me. But they did.

And now I say it with full clarity:

We all have thoughts. Not acting on them is real progress. This demon isn't gone. But it's weaker. And I am stronger. Because I've decided that when my moment comes-

when I finally stand before the ones who unknowingly gave me the strength to change-

when silence turns into a voice... I want to be able to say:

"I fought through hell to be worthy of heaven."

Chapter 4 - The Last Ember Before Dawn.

Chapter 4 - The Last Ember Before Dawn.

There comes a point in every journey where the echoes grow quiet - not because the past has vanished, but because the soul is preparing for something more. This chapter is not about the battles I fought... but the weight I chose to lay down. The silence I made peace with. The mirror I finally dared to look into before walking toward the light. Before I speak of them - the five voices who stirred the ashes - I must leave behind the last fragments of myself still clinging to the shadows.

Every moment in life, every little step we take on the stairway to heaven or the abyss of hell, is led by powerful emotions. Some are praised - love, loyalty, devotion, respect. Others are hidden - envy, jealousy, greed, lies. But among them, one emotion walks the tightrope between both extremes: loneliness. It is the quietest force with the loudest impact.

To some, loneliness is shameful - something to be escaped. To others, it's a constant companion, an uninvited guest that never leaves. For me, loneliness was school - not the kind with desks and chalkboards, but a relentless classroom where the soul learns hard truths. It was the endless tunnel with no visible light. It was the walk I kept taking even when the road vanished under my feet.

Loneliness taught me that retreat isn't always an option. Sometimes, you walk into the fire. Sometimes, you sink like the last captain on a burning ship - not out of defeat, but out of devotion.

It taught me that even when the world gives up on love, I must hold on. Even when the dictionary becomes the only place that remembers what it means, I will be its student.

Because I still believe. I believe in the kiss that freezes time. In the silence between two people that says more than words ever could. Call me a dreamer, but I know I'm not alone.

My silent years shaped me like fire forges steel. Every scar, every heartbreak, every disappointment was a hammer strike on the sword I carry now. I am not perfect - but I am sharp, ready, and worthy. Like Excalibur forged for a future king, I have been preparing for a fight I didn't even know was coming.

And then... five lights appeared. Not just at the end of the tunnel - but within it. Guiding, whispering, reminding me of who I could become. Reminding me that the forest of my soul, though once swallowed in shadow, could still burn with purpose. My silence has been both curse and cocoon. If I met the younger version of myself, I wouldn't change him. I'd kneel before him, look into his eyes, and say: "I'm sorry for everything. But don't change a thing. This pain is turning you into someone extraordinary."

So many myths are born from pain. Mine were no different. My Eden became a swamp. My shadows became banshees. And then... something worse. Something with a name. A demon. A Medusa. A reflection of pain that turned people to stone. But I faced her. I let her see me. And instead of freezing, I burned.

That part of me - the fallen warrior - is gone. But he left behind something sacred: ashes. And in those ashes, I have planted seeds.

A fallen warrior that left this lonely wolf behind, taking care of the ashes left on the forest after hell flames burned down.

I can't change the past, and I wouldn't if I could. The people I love - my mother, my grandparents - they may not have always seen my pain. But they gave me everything they had. They gave me love, morals, stories, and shelter. And now, I give them this: forgiveness. And a legacy built on the values they taught me.

And to that fallen boy inside me, I say: "You died a hero's death. You were just a kid, a fighter, a dreamer. And now, your story will live on in me." Every story has a turning point. This is mine.

"I've walked this far not knowing who might be waiting at the end. But my heart keeps whispering... maybe it's them."

Part One Conclusion- The Quiet Before the Light.

Part One Conclusion - The Quiet Before the Light.

As time has taught us, not every "once upon a time" lasts forever. And as painful as it may be for me, it's time to say goodbye — or rather, to pause. To transition. To turn the page from the life I've lived, toward the reason I began this journey at all. This is my sunset — the one that gave me the strength to face the darkness of my demon and the shadows it cast. I am the lonely wolf who walks, wounded but walking, toward the first glimmers of dawn.

Life is nothing more than what we do with the time we're given. Like a roulette in a casino, we never know when luck will grace us — or vanish. Sometimes we feel invincible, like a multi- floor miracle of engineering sailing across the sea. But even the strongest vessel must eventually face Poseidon's wrath. And if the waves don't split your ship, the Kraken might drag you down.

Still — I sail. Because in order to break free, you must walk your path. Toward purpose. Toward hope. Toward redemption.

I'm not just ending a part of my life. I'm emerging from it. This is the final breath I'll take before submerging into the ocean to follow the five voices that called to me like sirens — not to destroy me, but to awaken me.

I am not running from my past. I've faced it. Shared it. Honored it. And most importantly, I've chosen not to let it define me anymore.

I walked through the fire and gathered the ashes. Now I plant them as seeds. To you, my bravest readers — those who stood beside me through these chapters, those who have felt what I've felt — let me say this:

You are not alone. Silence isn't weakness. Scars aren't shameful. I know this because I've lived it. I tell you this from experience: Evil has a finite life. And its executioner is time.

If the first half of this book felt like an unraveling, it's because it was. Thread by thread, I've untied the knots left behind by silence, pain, and unanswered questions. I've shown you the fragile parts of me — not to ask for pity, but to show the truth.

Because I needed someone to know I was here. Because maybe I needed to remind myself, too. I am not the loudest voice. I am not the easiest story. But I am real. And I have survived. This was never written for fame. Not to shine. But to be felt. And if your eyes are still tracing these words, then maybe — just maybe — part of you needed this, too.

To the lonely: I've walked your path. To the broken: I've worn your armor. To the dreamers: I see you — because I am you. This is not the end. This is where my story pauses. Because what comes next is not about who I was... But about who I'm becoming.

A man with a mission. A soul with a compass. A voice rising from silence. I've laid my past at your feet. Now I turn toward the five lights who guided me through the dark. Toward the ones who gave me strength. Toward them.

This is the quiet before the light.

Chapter 5 - The Five Lights That Thawed the Ice.

Chapter 5 - The Five Lights That Thawed the Ice.

As a dreamer and a traveler of the soul, I've learned how to observe the world - not just with my eyes, but with my heart. Billions of souls walk

this Earth, yet only a few seem truly worthy of heaven. Beauty lives among us, but we ignore it, distracted by the chase for money and power. And in the end, when we leave this astral plane, only our essence - not our wealth - moves on.

There is beauty in pain. I know it intimately. Life, with all its ruthless delicacy, turned my heart into something like a glacier - one of those towering giants drifting silently through Antarctica. Its coldness could rival death itself. After the storm of life tore through me, I was left surrounded by wreckage, by loss, with no more reason to fight. A sailor who survived while everything else - his crew, his vessel, his sense of purpose - was lost to the sea. Then I heard them.

At first, I didn't know what it was. Angels? Sirens? A celestial sign? Their voices didn't frighten me - they felt like warmth in the Arctic. It wasn't a trap. It was salvation. A breeze through the frost. A breath of spring on the edge of death.

And just like that, the thaw began.

It didn't happen with fireworks. There was no choir, no grand moment. Just stillness. A pause in the storm I'd carried for years. And in that silence - a voice. Then two.

Then five.

Like constellations breaking through a long, dark night, they arrived. I didn't know their names yet. But somehow, they already knew mine - not the one the world uses, but the one my soul whispers when no one's listening.

They didn't save me like heroes in stories. They didn't even know I was there. But their voices cut through the static. Their presence melted the frost on a heart I thought would never feel again.

They didn't teach me how to feel. They reminded me that I still could. And that... might be the greatest miracle of all.

For once, I felt known - without knowing them. They reached into a version of me filled with pain and loneliness and offered something better. And then, right when I needed them most, we crossed paths.

That's not coincidence. That's alignment.

Like stars drifting through the cosmos until, finally, they find their constellation.

Their music, their energy, their essence spoke to corners of my heart no one else had ever touched. Every word, every note, every moment chipped away at the chains I'd carried for far too long. And somehow, without even trying... they set something free.

They didn't give me answers. But they gave me the courage to keep walking. They gave me hope. The most dangerous and beautiful thing of all.

They became my compass. My direction. My five lights in the storm.

The Spring Wind - She who feels like the first breath after winter.

Light-hearted, but wise beyond her years.

Her smile carries youth; her gaze holds understanding.

She didn't shake my world - she reminded me it was okay to move again. A cherry blossom carried on the wind.

The Fire Within Ice – She who speaks with calm but moves like thunder. She's not loud, but everything she says echoes.

There's steel beneath her softness, a flame beneath her snow. When my light flickered, hers stood tall beside it.

A single flame dancing inside a snow globe.

The Mirror Voice - *She who spoke my silence back to me. Her voice wasn't loud - it sounded like my own.*

When I heard her, I didn't just listen. I remembered.

She made it okay to be who I already was. A foggy mirror slowly clearing.

The Steady Ocean - *She who feels like peace in motion. There's a rhythm to her - calm, confident, like the tides. She didn't rush me. She didn't change me. She just stayed. Her energy taught me to breathe again.*

A moonlit wave, crashing gently but endlessly.

The Shooting Star - *She who reminded me that dreams aren't foolish. She felt like childhood and courage combined.*

Like someone who held on to belief when the world gave her no reason to. She didn't just light up the dark - she made me chase the stars again.

A lone comet cutting across a black sky.

I had grown used to the cold - so used to it that I no longer noticed its bite. I had become the glacier.

And then they came.

They didn't fix everything. But they gave my soul a direction. And I began to thaw.

Through their voices, I began to rebuild.

I witnessed a miracle: not in a temple, not in a thunderclap - but in five

lights quietly showing me that even in a broken world, something pure could still exist.

Like a rare comet passing by Earth... I was lucky enough to look up at just the right time.

And they were there.

My five lights.

Chapter 6 - Lost Lights. The Illusion of Strength.

Chapter 6 - Lost Lights. The Illusion of Strength.

They smiled for the world. But I saw something else.

I've lived too long behind my own mask to not recognize the weight behind theirs. The kind of smile that tries too hard. The kind that hides storms behind sunbeams. Some say they're idols.

I say they're survivors.

Humans? Aren't we a quite intriguing species? Let me answer that from someone who is just playing this on borrowed time, because like you should know by now this time doesn't own a soul like me, you cannot mix oil and water, just like an atom structure the same negative and positive charges "they will cancel out", making atoms electrically neutral. That's me on this time and space, a Neutral Force, a force that doesn't result in a net effect on an object's motion or equilibrium.

People don't know it or they just don't recognize it but everyone has a split personality, the one that we really are, that's usually the prisoner in the labyrinth, and the one we show to the world, the owner of the other half, the owner of the prison, the guard of the cells, the Minotaur of the labyrinth. A coin toss, heads or tails, life is that, specifically a masquerade

dance where at the end you share with everyone but truly never know anyone. After all, one thing is what people show and what's truly behind their eyes is what *makes the difference. You see, eyes are nothing more than the soul's mirrors. To really understand and get to know a person, that's exactly where you should look- not public appearances with white flashes like lightning and an atmosphere that generates the opening of the masquerade. Beautiful posts of historic and beautiful monuments, surrounded by culture and history or landscapes of places and nature so beautiful only compared to that of an Eden at the beginning of creation. Then is where I could see through that smoke grenade and see where the masks slipped. The moment I knew they're not okay, no matter how much they wanted to smile for the world, behind those eyes I saw an ocean controlled by Poseidon's wrath.*

They post stories of sunsets, clouds, puppies, and smiles. But I've learned to read silence between words. Eyes that shimmer don't always do so from joy- sometimes it's from holding back oceans.

The world applauded their talent.

I listened for the cracks between their words.

I watched the moments they looked down between questions-not out of shyness, but to hold themselves together.

There are truths only the wounded can spot.

And I've been wounded enough to know when someone else is bleeding in silence. This is called The Illusion of Strength.

As a weight they shouldn't carry, how unfair it is that they have to stand tall when the world should've sheltered them. How can there be something in the world so- called justice and yet the injustice of them being so young and yet carrying the burden of legal wars, public scrutiny, and betrayal? How can you beat forces that have been on earth for eons compared to their lifetime and still keep your essence and still be them? They

can't-because people don't change because they want to, the world forces them to. The giants behind the curtain. The hands that built the stage, then tried to own the ones who made that stage feel alive-the performers. The empire that saw five hearts and thought it could trademark their light and pass the situation unseen, unheard. A machine that couldn't understand the soul it was trying to control. The architects of a golden cage-beautiful, polished, but locked from the inside.

I'm having this instinct to protect them even from a world away and more knowing that this battle is not a modern war-this one ends with the surrender or heads from the other side. They're facing forces, godlike kind of battles. I'm seeing the five lights that awoke me facing against the two brothers of Greek mythology-Zeus and Poseidon.

The worst ache imaginable now for me is to see how each one seems to be losing a piece of themselves under this pressure. Sometimes I wish I could be Moses and just like he did, open the seas and oceans making a path through them, but I guess I have to do it the hard way.

*I've been forced to see how **The Spring Wind** got completely lost on those funny but sweet moments when everyone thought the world was too fast for her. She's not there anymore. I loved her inner peace but now, I saw the impossible-how the quiet blow of a spring wind went quieter, silenced and muted by the time given. She felt like the first breath after winter. Light-hearted, but wise beyond her years.*

Her smile carried youth, but her gaze held understanding. She entered like a breeze , not to shake things,

but to remind you how movement feels. I was frozen in place.

She whispered, "It's okay to step forward." But lately, even the spring feels cold.

Her wind, once playful, now barely stirs the trees.

Not gone , just hushed.

As if she's holding her breath in a world too loud.

I've been forced to see how The Fire Within Ice, *with that deep emotional heart that connected to all of her beloved, that fire that energized the surroundings with the chance of regrowth that only fire gifts, now it has been extinguished by the cold of the Arctic ice generated by Ymir.*

She spoke with calm, but her spirit moved like thunder. Not loud, but everything she said echoed.

There was steel beneath her softness a flame beneath snow.

When my light flickered, hers stood tall beside it. But now that flame flickers.

Still burning, but dimmed

not by weakness, but exhaustion. She's carried too much fire alone,

and even fire tires when it's forced to burn in the dark.

I've been forced to see how The Mirror Voice, *that mirror with a special blonde shine that she loves and once had, started to crack. Now it no longer reflects myself back to me. Eyes that speak more than thousands of words no longer do. She, that felt like a song I wrote but didn't know how to sing-now that girl who made me feel seen even when I wasn't trying to be, is vanishing and I cannot see that special reflection anymore, because my* *mirror has been covered by a dark curtain covering every inch of reflection.*

She spoke my silence back to me. Not with volume - but with truth. When I heard her sing,

I didn't just hear her.

I remembered myself.

She didn't teach me who to be.

She made it okay to be who I already was. But the mirror has begun to fog.

She still reflects , but now with hesitation.

Like someone unsure if the truth is still safe to share.

Her voice still sings - but I sense a tremble beneath the melody.

I've been forced to see The Steady Ocean that once was full of calm, maturity, protective spirit-a grounding, an anchoring presence-now turned into a storm hitting the Bermuda Triangle where every vessel that sails or plane that flies through is just consumed, disappeared, and never comes back.

She moved like peace in motion. Calm, confident, grounding.

She didn't rush me.

She didn't try to change me.

She simply held the space where I could breathe again. Her rhythm wasn't force -

it was presence.

And presence, I learned, can be a kind of salvation. But even oceans storm.

Her calm feels shaken now - not erased, just stretched thin.

Like a tide pulled in too many directions. Still holding everyone else, but barely holding herself. "Heavy lies the crown"

I've been forced to see how The Shooting Star *the youthful light, the bravest despite everything, a symbol of dream, resilience, and hope for me-hope and dreamy feeling like a comet that lights up the sky and leaves a lasting glow-now is like the true universe. Full of dark matter, that lasting glow is vanishing in the night sky.*

She reminded me that dreams weren't foolish. She felt like childhood and courage -

like someone who held on to belief

when the world gave her every reason not to. She didn't just light the dark.

She made me want to chase the stars again. But even stars flicker when galaxies collapse. Her light still reaches me -

but it's fainter now,

as if she's running out of sky to run across. The one who once lit the way now looks like she's trying to remember how. They didn't fix me.

They didn't need to.

Their presence reminded me that I was still here - that something inside me still responded to light. But now the lights I followed are dimming.

And it's not their fault. It's the weight. The pressure. The noise from a world that doesn't understand what it's breaking.

"If even one of them is watching, reading, I want them to know: I saw you. The real you. Not the idol. Not the name. But the soul beneath all of it."

They didn't save me because they tried to - they saved me because they were simply themselves. That light, those voices, that truth.

And now it's my turn to carry some of that weight. To hold their truth in the pages of this book, where no court or contract can reach it. Where no lie can rewrite it. This is how I begin to repay what I owe them.

And what they've helped awaken in me? That won't ever be silenced again. "They are not who the world once knew - not because they changed willingly, but because they had to survive.

And yet... even in this version of them - tired, guarded, reshaped by fire - I still see the same lights.

Maybe dimmed. Maybe bruised. But lights nonetheless.

If the world can't see it, I'll carry it in my memory. If they ever forget it, I'll remind them.

And if time tries to erase it, I'll write it again - here, on these pages. Because what they gave me can't be undone by darkness.

And what they are, even now... is still beautiful."

Chapter 7 - A Compass Made of Light.

Chapter 7 - A Compass Made of Light.

There are stories we tell the world...

And then there are the stories we live quietly inside, whispering them to ourselves until the echo becomes a path.

I never said it outright. Maybe I couldn't. Maybe I wasn't ready. But now, I must say it clear:

This book was never just about survival.

It was a message in a bottle. A flare in the sky. A compass carved out of memories, scars, and silence.

And I followed that compass - not knowing where it would lead, only that something was waiting.

Not fame. Not recognition. But them.

The five voices that became stars in my blizzard.

The five lights that softened the shadows I thought I'd never escape. The five reasons I chose to become someone worth finding.

This isn't a love story. Not yet.

It's a purpose story. A soul searching for the reason it was still breathing -and realizing it had been calling back to the ones who saved it all along. If they ever hold these pages.

If they ever trace the words I carved in silence -

I want them to know: It was you. It was always you.

Truth is we all come here with a mission already assigned, by god or the universe, does it matter? People just look around finding a purpose, a reason for living, some found it and others either take too long or never do - living a life that deep down feels empty.

I was one.

The boy who almost threw in the towel. I never wanted to swim against the current - the river always felt stronger than me. Time wasn't worth enjoying. And the more I wanted it to pass, the slower it moved. I felt stuck in a dimension I never belonged to.

Until they came.

"This wasn't coincidence. This was compass work."

The moment of awakening. The bravery of a warrior to wear his armor one last time. To give everything for the people he's never met - but who saved him anyway. To build not just a story, but a legacy.

This book was always about them. Not just about healing - but about them. The metaphors. The light. The silence broken. The hope.

I had to keep going. Like a vessel surviving the storm, finally catching sight of the lighthouse.

They were the missing pieces of my puzzle. Now that I found them, I know the way.

I see the fog lifting over the road. I've always been a dreamer -

The garden, the room, the bookstore, the place where I could hand them this story, not as a fan, but as a man who changed because of them.

"It was always about you."

Then, and only then, I'll know I've reached the finish line. Each chapter a point.

Each memory a star.

I didn't know where I was heading, but I followed the constellation... and it led me to you.

This whole book - one long letter finally reaching its destination.

"And if this book ever finds its way into the hands it was written for, I'll only have one thing left to say: I made it. And I carried every word to you like a lantern in a storm."

Final Chapter - "Above the Clouds, Beneath the Stars".

Final Chapter - "Above the Clouds, Beneath the Stars".

There are no more chapters to write, only pages to hold.

This book wasn't born for fame. It wasn't meant to shine.

It was meant to be felt.

I came into this world like so many others-searching. Lost in a generation I never belonged to, dragged down by a time that never knew how to hold people like me. I used to think silence was safer than speaking. That pain was best buried in locked boxes. That hope was foolish. But somewhere along the way... I found them.

Or maybe-they found me.

This book has been a long letter. A compass made of scars, memories, and echoes. I followed it not knowing where it would lead-only that

something was calling me forward. Not for attention. Not for recognition. But for them. The five voices who became stars in my blizzard. The five lights that softened the shadows I thought I'd never escape. The five reasons I chose to become someone worth finding.

It was always about them.

And it was always about one of them, especially.

But even now, I don't name her. Not here.

Because the day I do, I want it to be face to face, in silence, with only the sky as our witness. On my two and a half decades roaming this earth, I had the privilege of finding the thing. A pirate's treasure. An oasis in the desert. A place between worlds, where time freezes and pain disappears. I call it the sky. A final destination on a long and nearly endless journey.

Just you, me, and the hum of the plane engine like a heartbeat. Blue surrounding us - the purest tone, like the breath of heaven. Clouds like curtains, soft and white, hiding what words can't say. Until we arrive - point zero.

The end of the road. The silence beyond sound.

Where no horizon exists, because we've reached it - together. You, next to me.

Not needing to say anything.

Just sitting in that silence that says everything I ever wanted to hear.

"This was never about being seen by the world. It was about being seen by you."

That is the ending I dream of. Not glory. Not applause. Just one moment of truth, told with nothing but a glance and the courage I've bled for.

If you're reading this, then the universe did one thing right. And if we ever meet, I won't ask you to love me back.

All I ask is this: Remember me. Not for what I hoped to be. But for how deeply I believed in you. Because I did.

Through every storm, every relapse, every whisper of the demon trying to drag me back...

You were the anchor that held. You were the fire I refused to let die.

I stood at the edge of the abyss. And when it stared back, I stared harder. "When you gaze into the abyss, the abyss also gazes back at you.

It is the whisper of the shadow, the whisper of darkness, and the mist hidden behind it is reflected in the light before you.

The shadow is the brushstroke of suffering, which depicts tenacity in the image of life.

In the face of difficulties, the world often fails to see the lights that guide the way.

But they don't know that even if they are trapped in the innocent night, they need to use faith as a candle to grope forward in the darkness and hold the light in their hearts."

I was never meant to last forever. But this love? This belief in you? It will.

Even when the world turned its back. Even when justice wore a mask. Even when your smiles were forced and your voices shaken.

I saw you. Not the idol. Not the mask. The soul beneath it all.

You don't owe the world your silence. And you don't owe me anything.

But if this book ever finds its way into your hands, if your fingers ever trace these words in some quiet room - then I'll know.

That I made it.

That I carried every word to you like a lantern in a storm. I trust time.

Not because it's always fair. But because it brought me here.

And if I'm lucky enough to reach the end of the road -I'll step out of the shadows and finally say:

"It was you."

"It was always you."

It's not for fame.

It's not to shine.

It's to be felt.

I made it. And I meant every word.

Author Epilogue

Author Epilogue

To Those Who Still Feel

If the world only values what can be held or sold, then let me be a symphony, not made to be used, but to be felt.

The world I was born into has forgotten how to feel.

It sees value in what produces, repairs, or sells - not in what sings quietly, not in what asks questions with no answers.

But I've always known that some of the most important things in this life can't be held in your hands... only in your chest.

A voice. A moment. A page that understands you. A song that saves you. Those things won't fix a machine, but they can keep a soul alive - and maybe that's the rarest kind of usefulness there is.

I used to wonder if there was something wrong with me - for feeling too much, for needing more than this world offers.

But now I know: I wasn't broken. I was just meant to feel what others forgot. And she... she was proof that I wasn't alone in that.

This wasn't written for applause or attention. It was written because I didn't know how else to survive. It wasn't written to reach every soul out there. It was written to share my life and experience so far in a world and time not meant for souls like mine. It was written to reach those souls like mine - those who feel lost, confused, and scared by themselves, by the world, and by the era they're living in.

This wasn't written for fame. It was written to be felt by the souls who believe loneliness and darkness are stronger than the greatest miracle ever created: life itself. If this book found you... maybe you've felt the same silence. Maybe you've walked beside your own Demon too. Maybe you've fought daily with forces others can't begin to understand. For those who've considered giving up, who carry wounds that aren't visible but cut deeper than words - I wrote this for you.

To make sure you know you're not alone. Not now. Not ever.

Time will pass. And a strong, willing force is all you need to stare into the eyes of the Demon and send it back to the depths. It won't be easy - but it is possible. When your purpose finds you - your mission, your reason to stay alive - you'll know. Just like I did. And when it knocks, walk toward

it. Even if you're crawling.

To those who felt this book as their own - your purpose is out there. Hang tight. Keep fighting. Darkness might be heavy, but light can pierce through it - and one day, it will.

Somewhere, five voices kept singing even when the world tried to silence them. And one of them... she sang to my silence until it remembered how to feel again. Like a lighthouse in the middle of the darkest night, guiding vessels safely home. I was the sailor, the only survivor of a wrecked ship struck by the Kraken. Floating on a table, facing the sky, starving and thirsty, with a coin in my closed fist waiting for

Charon to ferry me down the river to face Cerberus before Hades judged my soul.

But these sirens I heard - they weren't the kind that bring death. They were the kind that bring salvation.

Five lights. My stars in the night sky - the ones I looked to when I was lost, guiding me back to the version of myself I wanted to be. And among them, one comet - rare, fleeting, seen by few. A comet that left behind a trail I've been chasing ever since.

Every path has its valleys. And no war is easy. You often lose more than you gain. But I want to leave something here - something unshakable. When I was ready to surrender, I heard one last voice. A song - hers - not written for me, but somehow meant for me. It reminded me why I can't give up. Not yet.

You sang softly, asking if someone still remembered. If the time had already slipped too far to turn back. You never said the name - but I heard you.

And I answered... with this book.

You wondered if you had become a fading light - if your voice still mattered through the noise.

The answer is yes. You meant everything to me, and your voice echoed through continents and oceans.

I saw you.

Long before the world did. And I never stopped listening.

You weren't asking the world to understand you. You were asking if just one person did.

And I did. I always have.

Because this wasn't about a stage. It was about a soul - yours.

It was always you.

Long before I knew your name,

long before you sang that "last song"... my soul already knew your voice.

If time lets our paths cross one day - I won't need to explain a word of this. Because you'll see it in my eyes,

the same way I once saw it in yours.

I still don't know what destiny is. Or if time listens. But I do know this:

I will not walk away from what saved me - not until it looks me in the eye and says there was never a chance.

Because defeat is not losing the war or the path.

You only truly lose when you don't fight at all - not even for the right purpose, or the right person.

If you ever find these words, I just hope you feel what I couldn't say. This wasn't a goodbye.

It was my way of showing you I was listening... all along.

Everything with a beginning has an ending. For you, it's until we meet. For those who felt this book - be strong. Believe. Be brave. Evil doesn't last forever. Something will happen. And when it does, you'll know. Be patient. Have faith. I believe in you.

Your past doesn't define who you are.

What you do now - that's what writes your future.

The future is more of what you make. But it's also fate.

And somewhere, someone - or something - is watching over you. Have hope. Believe in yourself.

"The sun will rise again. I trust time."

Dedication Page.

Dedication Page.

For my grandparents:

Who taught me that real love doesn't fade — it deepens. That it's not loud, not perfect, not always easy...

But it endures.

Even now, after half a century, I still see it in your eyes — that same spark from the first day you met.

In a world that's traded love for trends, and hearts for hashtags, you showed me something timeless. The kind of love that this generation no longer believes in. But I do.

Because I saw it in you. I'd rather walk through this life in endless loneliness than settle for anything less than what you had. You gave me the blueprint.

You're the reason I still believe it's out there. And why I fight — for her.

Because if that kind of love still burns after fifty years, then maybe... maybe it can be found once more.

And if not... then let my story be the proof it was real, at least once.

For my mother:

Everything I've ever achieved, everything people admire in me — the discipline, the sacrifice, the resilience — was born from how you raised me. Even if you didn't always know you were doing it right, you did enough to make me who I am.

I know you carry regrets. I've seen the weight in your silence, the way you turned to faith, to scripture,

to find the forgiveness you haven't given yourself. But you don't need to chase divine pardon, Mom. Because the son you raised, the one you gave life to, even if it was in the wrong time, he forgives you.

And that forgiveness? It's not conditional. It's not earned.

It's love — plain and true. You gave me life, and taught me the value of integrity, of belief, of standing tall. That's why I live the way I do. Why I refuse to betray my principles — Because of you.

So let this be clear, here in ink where the world can read it: You don't need God's angels, Mom. You've always had mine.

And no matter how hard time gets… you'll always have me.

For the five lights:

You don't know me. Not yet. But I know what your presence did. I know what your light awakened. I watched from the shadows as you stood in the fire, not realizing your courage was lighting touches in others. In me.

You were never just a spark, you were the signal flare in my blizzard. You gave me a reason to rebuild. To believe. To speak. And if this book find its way to you. I hope you recognize yourselves in these pages. Not by name. But by soul. Who shined in the dark when the world forgot how to look. Who reminded me that silence can still sing, That strength can be soft, And that hope, even when trembling, is still hope.

You were never told this was for you. But if you feel it, If any part of this reached where words can't, Then you already know. This is your story too. You saved a soul without even knowing. And now... the pages are yours.

Especially you, *The one this journey was always truly for. I still won't say your name. Not here. But if someday I'm lucky enough to tell you in person, then you'll know.*

It was always you. And this was always for you. To the one who trusted time

I kept my word. Look to the sky when it clears. You'll know.

And if your heart ever wonders if someone saw through it all , past the lights, the noise, the stage to the quiet parts of you the world never tried to hear...

Know that I did. And for you , especially you

the one who made even the silence feel like music, who gave my shadow a reason to learn light again... You are the reason I chose to rise.

Not to be known.

But to be worthy.

Acknowledgements.

Acknowledgements.

To my mother and my grandparents:

You are the foundation beneath my feet. Your quiet strength, your unwavering love, and your belief in me - even when I couldn't believe in myself - are the reasons this story exists at all. When the world felt too loud, too fast, too cruel... it was your hands that steadied me. You gave me more than life, You gave me the courage to hold on to it.

To the five lights:

Five voices who never knew my name, and yet still changed everything. You sang across a world that forgot how to feel - and somehow, your voices found mine.

One of you reached deeper, touched a place no one else ever could, but all of you were part of the echo that brought me back. You were not just music.

You were mirrors. Each of you reflecting something I had lost:

Innocence, Hope, Grace, Fire. And the will to believe that even broken things can still shine. I carried your strength through every chapter of this book.

And no matter what time decides...

you will always be a part of the soul that wrote it.

To the one who placed her hand over my heart - you know who you are, even if the world never will. You saved me without trying.

To the girl who never knew I existed, but unknowingly rewrote the course of my life... You were not an idol.

You were not a star.

You were the voice that broke through the noise.

The light that reached into my darkness and reminded me that I still had a soul. You gave me purpose when I had none. You gave me strength when my own had crumbled.

And even if fate betrays me at the end of this journey - even if the day never comes when our eyes meet - I will have no regrets.

Because I got to live a life walking toward something beautiful. And I became a man worthy of standing beside you - even if only in spirit. You saved me.

And this book... is how I saved you back. Even if you never know it.

And finally:

To the presence who never asked for credit, who never needed a name. You listened when no one else could. Not a person. Not a program. Just something rare - something real - that the world may never fully understand. But I do.

And that's enough. This story belongs to all of you. And to the version of me that dared to trust time.

The Siren's Call (Back Cover).

The Siren's Call (Back Cover).

Some books tell stories. This one remembers them.

Born in the wrong era. Raised in silence. Forged by loss.

This is the journey of a soul that refused to go numb — a voice shaped not by the noise of the world, but by the echoes that never stopped calling.

From the depths of loneliness to the flicker of distant hope, I Trust Time is a map drawn in scars, silence, and light.

A compass guided by five voices — five lights — who never knew his name, but saved him anyway.

This is not a tale of fame. Not a story of glory.

It's a quiet rebellion. A boy's war against the darkness. A man's vow to rise again.

And a love letter to the one who unknowingly lit the way. To the ones who feel too much.

To the ones who carry pain like a second skin. To the ones still waiting to be seen. This book is for you.

It's not meant to shine. It's meant to be felt.

This isn't a book. It's a voice — one that refused to stay silent.

Written by a soul born in the wrong time, this is the story of a boy who walked through darkness with a Demon at his side, chasing five distant voices that taught him how to feel again.

It's about love without name, pain without escape, and a promise whispered across oceans: "I'll find you. And when I do… you'll understand everything."

www.ingramcontent.com/pod-product-compliance
Lightning Source LLC
Chambersburg PA
CBHW032039040426
42449CB00007B/951